Bounding

for

Light

A Children's Poetry Anthology

Compiled & Edited by Richard Mbuthia

Mwanaka Media and Publishing Pvt Ltd,
Chitungwiza Zimbabwe

*

Creativity, Wisdom and Beauty

Publisher:

Mmap

Mwanaka Media and Publishing Pvt Ltd

24 Svosve Road, Zengeza 1

Chitungwiza Zimbabwe

mwanaka@yahoo.com

https://mwanakamediaandpublishing.weebly.com

Distributed in and outside N. America by African Books Collective

orders@africanbookscollective.com

www.africanbookscollective.com

ISBN: 978-0-7974-9332-2

EAN: 9780797493322

DISCLAIMER

All views expressed in this publication are those of the author and do not necessarily reflect the views of *Mmap*.

Contents Table

v

v

Bio Notes of Contributors

NAMARA Lwansa: She is 11 years old. Her hobbies are dancing, reading and poetry writing. She would like to grow into a responsible, productive and independent person. Ambition: To be a journalist. *Namara was the third place winner in a nationwide poetry writing competition in Tanzania (August 2018) dubbed "A Poem for Peace". The competition was organized by The American Embassy, Soma Book Café and Waka Poetry Consortium.*

 FAUTIA Mogaeka: She is 12 years old. Her hobbies are: reading, poetry writing and singing. She would like to grow up to be an industrious and responsible African citizen who respects and helps the poor and needy. Ambition: To become a Scientist. *Fautia was among the fifty best poets in a nationwide poetry writing competition in Tanzania (August 2018) dubbed "A Poem for Peace". The competition was organized by The American Embassy, Soma Book Café and Waka Poetry Consortium.*

 IAN Richard: He is 12 years old. His hobbies are singing, dancing and acting. He would like to grow into a kind-hearted, caring, assertive and confident African. Ambition: To be a scientist. *Ian was among the fifty best poets in a nationwide poetry writing competition in Tanzania (August 2018) dubbed "A Poem For Peace". The competition was organized by The American Embassy, Soma Book Café and Waka Poetry Consortium.*

 NICOLE Kamando: She is 11 years old. Her hobbies are watching TV, designing and singing. She would like to grow into a beautiful, God-fearing, kind and industrious woman. Ambition: To be a scientist. *Nicole was among the fifty best poets in a nationwide poetry writing competition in Tanzania (August 2018) dubbed "A Poem For Peace". The competition was organized by The American Embassy, Soma Book Café and Waka Poetry Consortium.*

HARRISON Robert: He is 12 years old. His hobbies are playing football, watching TV and watching video games. He would like to grow up to be an African who cares and is compassionate to the sick. Ambition: To become a Doctor.

WILLYHELM Shayo: He is 13 years old. His hobbies are playing football and singing. He would like to grow up into a kind-hearted person who is polite and respects everybody. Ambition: To become a pilot.

JAMES Uria: He is 13 years old. His hobbies are playing piano and singing. He would like to grow up into a faithful and honest person. Ambition: To become a communications engineer.

SALHIA Mchatta: She is 10 years old. Her hobby is reading. She would like to grow up into a kind and caring person. Ambition: To be an entrepreneur.

CHELSEA Ilumba: She is 11 years old. Her hobbies are reading, gymnastics, and spending time with friends. She would like to grow into a person who respects and helps others. Ambition: To be an engineer.

IRENEY Ngayama: She is 11 years old. Her hobbies are participating in sports, reading stories, dancing and singing. She would like to grow up into a responsible person who cares for and helps the needy. Ambition: To be a lawyer.

ANGEL Mgaya: She is 11 years old. Her hobbies are singing, dancing, riding and reading story books. She would like to grow up into a person who will make the world a better place. Ambition: To be a lawyer.

PRINCESSIA Mrema: She is 12 years old. Her hobbies are singing, reading story books, dancing. She would like to grow into a person who helps the poor and needy and make her parents proud in all that she does. Ambition: To be a business woman.

JANIYAH Abbas: She is 12 years old. Her hobbies are singing, dancing, writing poems, reading story books and swimming. She would like to grow up into an African citizen who respects others. Ambition: To be a business woman.

FARIDA Yahya: She is 13 years old. Her hobbies are participating in sports, singing, dancing and reading story books. She would like to grow up into a respectful and responsible person. Ambition: To be an air hostess.

NAINKWA Mbati: She is 12 years old. Her hobbies are singing and cooking. She would like to grow up into a compassionate and kind African citizen. She would like to pursue her education to PhD level. Ambition: To be a paediatrician.

LUBANGO Wangwe: He is 12 years old. His hobbies are playing games, reading and watching TV. He aspires to be a role model to others and a person who does not break other people's peace. Ambition: To be a surgeon.

HENRY Humphrey: He is 12 years old. His hobbies are drawing and taking part in athletics. He would like to grow up into a respected and honest man. Ambition: To be a pilot.

NATHANIEL Ondigo: He is 13 years old. His hobby is reading story books. He wants to grow up into a kind and respected man. Ambition: To be a lawyer.

CHRISTINA Mlay: She is 13 years old. Her hobbies are dancing and swimming. She wants to be a kind and responsible person who will be ready to defend her country. Ambition: To be a lawyer.

ANJELITHA Michael: She is 13 years old. Her hobby is cooking. She wants to grow up into a responsible, honest and hardworking person who respects others. Ambition: To be a lawyer.

JOHANNES Lewis: He is 13 years old. His hobby is playing football and watching TV. He wants to grow up into a kind, humble and respected person. Ambition: To be an accountant.

NATHAN Kamando: He is 11 years old. His hobbies are playing football, playing piano and watching TV. He would like to grow up into a respected person. Ambition: To be an entrepreneur.

GLORY Fadhili: She is 12 years old. Her hobbies are swimming and adventure. She would like to grow up into an author of adventure books, a kind and loving mother and a citizen who helps in the development of Africa. Ambition: To be an engineer.

VIDA Mapunda: She is 11 years old. Her hobby is singing. She would like to grow up into a faithful person who helps the poor people of Africa. Ambition: To be a gynaecologist.

VINNA Frank: She is 11 years old. Her hobbies are singing and dancing. She would like to grow into an activist who fights for women's rights. Ambition: To be a lawyer.

JONATHAN Kezirahabi: He is 12 years old. His hobbies are playing football and watching TV. He would like to grow up into a kind and respected person in society. Ambition: To be an entrepreneur.

PRECIOUS Mwageni: She is 12 years old. Her hobbies are writing and singing. She would like to grow up into a hardworking and respected person. Ambition: To be a pilot.

DAVYNN Faraja: She is 11 years old. Her hobbies are singing, swimming, reading and poetry writing. She would like to grow up into an honest, faithful and loving woman who believes in God. Ambition: To be an entrepreneur.

KAYDEN Prosper: He is 12 years old. His hobbies are reading, playing football and watching TV. He would like to grow up into an honest person who serves God and humanity. Ambition: To be an architect.

SIA Izumbe: She is 11 years old. Her hobbies are swimming, dancing and watching TV. She would like to grow into a person who respects people and God. Ambition: To be a doctor.

MERCY-Anna Kijazi: She is 12 years old. Her hobbies are reading, singing and poetry writing. She would like to grow into a caring woman who trusts in God. Ambition: To be an entrepreneur.

ZILPA Mkama: She is 12 years old. Her hobbies are swimming, rapping and standup comedy. She would like to grow into an assertive and God-fearing individual. Ambition: To be a cardiologist.

DOREEN Mosha: She is 14 years old. Her hobbies are singing and swimming. She would like to grow into an honest, generous and help people who are in need. Ambition: To be an entrepreneur.

NICOLE Oscar: He is 12 years old. Her hobbies are listening to music, dancing and taking part in sports. She would like to grow up into an honest and helpful person. Ambition: To be a lawyer.

GRACE Bwire: She is 12 years old. Her hobby is writing mashairi (Kiswahili poetry). She would like to grow into a caring and responsible citizen of the world. Ambition: To be a doctor.

JOANNE Mteteri: She is 12 years old. Her hobby is drawing, singing and reading. She wants to grow into a responsible citizen of Africa. Ambition: To be a scientist.

JASMINE Kapya: She is 12 years old. Her hobbies are reading, writing, taking part in science experiments and listening to music. She would like to grow into a humble and committed individual out to change Africa and the world for the better. Ambition: Neurosurgeon.

PETER Lumumba: He is 13 years old. His hobbies are dancing, singing, watching TV, playing football. He would like to grow into a person who is compassionate about the plight of the poor. Ambition: To be an engineer.

GRAYSON Kamukala: He is 14 years old. His hobbies are singing, dancing and playing basketball. He would like to grow into a responsible person and offer help to the needy. Ambition: To be an engineer.

RICHARD Daniel: He is 12 years old. His hobbies are playing football and dancing. He would like to grow into a hardworking person who helps the poor. Ambition: To be an entrepreneur.

SHILOH Kiluwasha: She is 12 years old. Her hobbies are sightseeing and reading. She would like to grow into a hardworking and faithful citizen of Africa. Ambition: To be a biologist.

IRENE Hanai: She is 12 years old. Her hobbies are reading story books, singing and watching TV. She would like to grow into a kind, caring and truthful person. Ambition: To be an entrepreneur.

SHARON Ayittah: She is 13 years old. Her hobbies are reading novels, watching TV and writing poems. She would like to grow up into a successful, God-fearing lady. Ambition: To be an entrepreneur.

DERRICK Massao: He is 12 years old. His hobbies are watching TV, listening to music and playing football. He would like to grow up into a successful man. Ambition: To be a doctor.

EILEEN Kitauli: She is 13 years old. Her hobbies are singing and dancing. She would like to grow into a responsible person. Ambition: To be a veterinarian.

STEVEN Kidindima: He is 13 years old. His hobby is playing football. He would like to grow into a faithful and responsible person who helps solve people's problems. Ambition: To be an entrepreneur.

Introduction

Working closely with the pupils whose poems appear in this collection, has been a great pleasure. It has been a journey with many worthy lessons. It has taught me that the young, too, have burning aspirations and dreams that should never be dismissed or snuffed out. Instead, they should be patiently nurtured and watered.

The poems in this collection are the pupils' own creations. The word choices and the images painted in the pieces are a crafting of the poets themselves.

The poems mirror the children's own aspirations, dreams, fears, day dreams and takes on different issues that affect their lives (even remotely). The pieces give wings to their inner voices – voices that at times are stifled. They give freedom to the inner spirit to soar and perch on the choicest branches and take in the sights.

As you read the pieces herein just know you are reading the works of future literature icons and enthusiasts. These are people who will shape the reading and writing trajectory of the nation; people who will initiate discussions of absolute import in the value of the written word. This is no mean feat.

For these pupils, the sky is not the limit – it is the starting point.
Richard Mbuthia, Editor

Closed Door

Joanne Mteteri, Anjelitha, Shiloh, Johannes

I see a crack
That shows me a track
That won't take me back
That gives me good luck.

I hear a creaking sound
That is in my head even loud
Give me a sign
Of what is behind.

I see a beam of light
That is out of my sight
That is not bright
Why can't you show me the light?

We open the window when the doors close
We extinguish a fire with a hose
We drink our medicine according to our dose
We try to win when we lose.

Everything has a solution
According to its proportion
As soon as everyone takes a portion
We will come up with a conclusion.

I see a structure

That represents my future
It was once darkened
But now the door is opened.

What if a dog could talk?

Jasmine Kapya, Richard, Nathan, Grayson, Christina

What if a dog could talk?
I think the world would stop
Oh, what utter nuisance
The world could lose its balance.

What if a dog could talk?
Would it also start to walk?
Would its effects turn back clocks?
Or would it automatically turn people into blocks?

What if a dog could talk
Would heaven's door lock?
Or would evil still mock
Or would pagans go to the hell door and knock.

What if a dog could talk
It would be a real joke
I probably should go to the doc
To people's opinion it sounds like a hoax.

To talk or not to talk that is the question
Would we actually start a conversation

Or go against God's creation
Would leaders now guide the people with hesitation?
And would dogs start having international integration.

I might be turning into a dog
Or I may be making a blog
Because I think I am going crazy
Or is it me thinking lazy?

Imagine huskies, Chihuahuas and bulldogs as presidents
So it means that their dog statehouse would be their residence
Am I actually speaking sense?
Would this effect make a good presence?

My conclusion is that this would change the world
And all the dogs' secrets would unfold
So that they wouldn't be left in the cold
Or cry that they have been sold.

A Farewell Forever

Jasmine Kapya, Richard, Nathan, Grayson, Christina

The word we promised not to say
Even on our last day
The word that carries so much sorrow
Like there will be no tomorrow.

It was a great pleasure for us to be together
But we might not see one another ever again
They say great thinking comes when great thoughts are shared
But the thought of saying that word is too much to bear.

You taught us that it takes courage to face reality
And that our commitment determines the quality of our destiny
You provided the utmost inspiration
Now we can face the world without temptation.

We'll never let go of your laudable words
That we were lucky even to afford,
We give you great appreciation
For that you've placed us in the right destination.

You've showered us with love's embellishment
And corrected us with encouragement
You've taught us so well
But still we don't think it's time for a farewell.

The tough times
The endless cries

And then suddenly a relieved sigh
But we still don't want to say goodbye.

You say, what hurts instructs
You've nurtured us as your own
For we are now self reliable
And made us mature and responsible.

We promised not to let you down
Neither shall we make you frown
For that we leave with half our heart
But no distance will tear us apart.

This experience was such a prize
That our success was in all shapes and sizes
For that our lives will essentially dwell
And this is our precious farewell.

Strange Conversation

Ian Richard, Irene, Jonathan, Doreen

How strange it is to talk to you
While I don't even know your name?
Why should I act like a fool to you
Yet I'm not even your close friend
How strange it is to talk to you
While I don't even know your name

I was travelling in a bus
Sitting next to me was a strong-looking man
Covered from top to bottom ninja style
Looking at me with a red eye, full of stress.

Passing through the streets enjoying my lifetime
A stranger talking to you bitterness through his eyes
Shivering through my soul talking to my mind
When I see this conversation I see a black coal
Talking back and forth, the intensity searing my soul.

Through the mystery of mysteries
I discover this man through that conversation
The moment I see a mad man
Talking through my heart like a terror
Thinking like I am talking to an emotionless man.

All that you tell me is unknown
I'm starting to think I was left alone
As chills run down my spine

When I hear your heavy voice booming my ear drum
Like a clock starting to chime
For, to me, time is not running out.

Now that we're reaching the stop
It shows me a big sign
For sooner your boring words will stop
It won't take long; it's almost the end of time.

Untouchable

Davynn Faraja, Grace, Kayden, Nicole Oscar, Vida

You thought I was broken
You thought my courage was stolen
You thought I couldn't do the impossible
You thought I am not reliable
But let me tell you darling, I'm more than untouchable.

You thought you could lie to me
You thought that I could not see
But I'm smarter than you, so let me be
You thought that you were capable
Of pretending that you were able.

You thought that you were tough
And oddly rough
A hands-on buff
You thought you could do all the stuff
And keep everything in touch.

I can't be touched
Like a chick that's just hatched
I know you want me
But you can't have this
It is super special; for it's out of reach.

I am untouchable
I am also believable
And surely unstoppable

Just know I will end up terrible
For sure untouchable is my name.

I am not despicable
Simply irresistible
Ravishing and sustainable
Very attractive but unstoppable
I am always untouchable.

Time Freeze

Glory Fadhili, Peter, Nathaniel, Eileen

Comes a time when everything stops
Everything turns into a shock
And every clock stops going tick tock
Sometimes you feel you are getting a stroke.

You feel like running away
But you can't you just have to stay
You try to look for a navigable way
On the world's last day.

Time freeze is like a breeze
Which can give you a brain freeze
In a channel full of bees
Like peanut butter and cheese.

Life with time freeze would be better
Because there would be no hater
Who could pretend and be a faker
But God will still be our creator.

Maybe you commit a crime
All the clocks stop chiming
You even lose the words to rhyme
When it's time to go to bed.

Time's fight is tight
Can divide the earth apart

Just when the blind gets sight
And the wicked are filled with fright.

When the time is freezing
It becomes confusing
When the days of living are decreasing
Sometimes you feel like skipping.

When you've done something wrong
The heartbeat is just strong
Time freeze can also go wrong
Like a sabotage of a song.

Absentee Father

Nicole Kamando, Sia, James, Henry

Father's footsteps for the first time today
Coming home, 'Open the door,' he says
Mum tells us, 'Don't worry, there is always a way'
The way now is to God we pray;
The absentee fathers shouldn't make the light ray
And kill us with whatever they say.

Did he have to be my father?
To look after me and my brother?
Taking care of the family, he doesn't even bother
Him, I'd rather have
As dad not as a father.

He left mom and I to brave it on our own
He turned the family upside down
In the life pool he made us drown
And filled us with frowns
Who gave him the crown
To cook us like prawns?

He broke my mother's heart
And the family came apart
He calls himself a priceless piece of art
The way he brags like the sound of a fart
He never does his part
And drives us like a cart.

He is a total abomination
He is the cause of the family's destruction
In family meetings he does zero cooperation
With his attitude he will never become father of the nation
For his is a terrible foundation
Invested in non-communication.

Locked in a Jar

Nicole Kamando, Sia, James, Henry

The feeling of being locked in a jar
Like the desire of wanting a chocolate bar
Even better than winning a new car
And a load of money to fix the road's tar
That's like some miles far
Why am I locked in a jar?

Outside, oh the lovely satisfaction
With undeniable attraction
Of the food that's just a fraction
but I have much consternation
While listening to the outdoor commotion
I am filled with a lot of emotion.

The best of joy is strolling
To a perfect place for strolling
Where the maggots are patrolling
If a wondrous smell is growing
And I see a balloon that is glowing
Then I know it's time for going.

Later strangely, I see a man from Spain
Riding in a train
A moment later he gets a sprain
And feels a lot of pain
I yell at him: No pain
No coloured gain.

I miss the light outside
The light that has pride
To God, I now abide
It is up to me to decide
To see the ocean tide
Or stay stuck inside.

The Consequences of War

Fautia Mogaeka, Precious, Willyhelm, Harrison

In the middle of a war
When the Earth is shaken till it's sore
People, full of rage
As if they're trapped inside a cage
Kick out the advice of a sage.

People are murdering
Some are isolating
Others are torturing
But children suffer
And there's no one there to buffer.

It's a very big disaster
That's worse than thunder;
Apart from war, we get refugees
And for someone who's not a smoker
Will hear them scream "Help me."

And the refugees experience hunger
That makes them lose their laughter
Truly this is a bad matter
That's gone worse to a disaster-here-after
And it has grown into a monster.

Children are caught up in this mess
Something which is a very big case
That doesn't even bother people, they are less,
Children are sunken in the valley of doubt
Are they ever going to get out?

Children are also affected in war and family struggle
And twists of life to make them paddle
They have to learn to juggle
As they seek motherly love –
They await the landing of that cute dove.

Death, a Fate
Namara Lwansa, Vinna, Steven, Lubango

Is there an afterlife?
Do you revive?
What is this fearful feeling?
Does it have a meaning?

Some are excited
Delighted even
Most of us fear
Is it coming? Is it here?

Is what we do partial?
is our life our commercial?
Reaching a conclusion
That is really an illusion.

It is the sudden end
How can we pretend
It is not you to decide
For you're in for a ride.

When you realize
You didn't organize
It's too late
Just wait for the pearly gates.

We don't have a choice
We can't use our voice

It will just happen
Like how fruits ripen.

It comes as a surprise
I don't think it has a price
You are driving a car suddenly an accident
Actually, it is not a punishment.

What is it?
It's death
Something all of us will face
When we breathe our last breath.

99999 0 g e 9

Silence

Namara Lwansa, Vinna, Steven, Lubango

Silence, the complete absence of sound
It sometimes sticks around
Silence is ambiguous
It could be continuous.

The brain can think when there is silence
Silence is often used to avoid violence
Silence is golden
Its meaning is folded.

When I am in silence, I get to think
Silence can instantly disappear before I blink
Even for a short moment silence is good
I wouldn't give it away for anything even if I could.

Don't take someone's silence
As their weakness is scalding
They just want to get aggressive
They want to go balding.

Another thing about silence
It's so unique
That the brain can't take it
You know how?

Have you ever been silent?
And heard a ringing so violent

It's called tinnitus
Shocking for the both of us.

Silence is broken
When one word is dropped
Silence is resilient
It is also resistant.

Lack of noise

Not a single voice
It is a great feeling
But I don't understand its meaning.

Eye Contact

Joanne Mteteri, Anjelitha, Shiloh, Johannes

When I look at you
I get a feeling that I can never despise
That leaves me hypnotized
A feeling that I can never criticize.

Time seems to stop
And you seem to be on the top
On top of my mind
That I can never dismiss.

I get you definition
In my imagination
Which brings up fusions
That cause illusions.

When I look at you I see a spark
That makes me see in the dark
Something that I will never lack
And I'll never turn back.

Time seems to fly
Like clouds up in the sky
Above mountains so high
As sweet as strawberry pie.

My heart seems to skip a beat
Whenever I see you look neat

I wish someday we could meet
In utmost reality.

The sky is blue
All I see is you
Violets are blue
Oh! What a wonderful hue.

This wonderful feeling
That is so thrilling
Oh, so fulfilling
The beautiful eye contact.

Love

Glory Fadhili, Eileen, Nathaniel, Peter

Love is a feeling
That brings down a thrilling
it's so spine chilling
Its feeling is so drilling.

It can feel casual or
Come about unusual
It's really gradual
Its streets in number are dual.

It's not extraterrestrial
it's not really comprehendible
it can guide you to six by four
Though you never thought about it before.

Love can send out fear
Love is a never ending sphere
So pure, so clear – its voice
Is loud and clear
It can clear things that you'll never hear.

Why is love like a spear
That can pass through a cracked sphere?
Some want to have love
Some even starve for love.

It can make you starve
And spin around in a curve
When in love you can forget
What you were to get.

Love is quality
When it comes to reality
Takes over your mentality
And also your creativity.

Do you have to go up to the skies
Using lofty ice skates
To realize ever so memorably
That love is nice?

Ode to My Favourite Colour

Sharon Ayittah, Zilpa, Mercy-Anna, Derrick

I dedicate this to you my colour
You're night and bright
You make my mood upright
You also make me all right
What a wonderful colour!

You give me a happy mood
Which to most people is good
You are so swell
In my clothes you dwell
What a beautiful colour!

You are an interesting colour
You bring a good sense of humour
If I were to paint on a wall
you will be on it all
What a soothing colour!

You are the colour of my bedspread
The comfortable bed
You are on my attire
For you are the one I admire
What a beautiful colour!

Sometimes you motivate me
To be the best I could ever be
Even though you are just a colour

You sometimes have surprising favour
What a beautiful colour!

What a beautiful colour you are
You sometimes put me at ease
When I lie on my bed
I think of the shimmering
Hot-blooded red.

Numbness

Sharon Ayittah, Zilpa, Mercy-Anna, Derrick

There's a weird feeling I get
Not feeling anything at all
It is very disconcerting
To go through this condition.

I feel jealous
When I see friends having fun
Missing time that is precious
Just lying here without seeing the sun.

I feel oddly at a loss
Not able to do anything
It's like I am paralysed
Or my spine's stopped working.

Missing the precious time
When I want to do something

But I can't feel anything
God have mercy on me.

Sometimes you don't have emotions
Not able to translate information
It is really a bad condition
To be utterly numb.

It's like a tyrant
Taking away your feeling
Waiting to be overthrown
It's an endless torture.

This feeling is so unfortunate
It gets away with your expression
It is unreliable unlike an emergency service
This is what you go through when you are numb.

It's like an episode that doesn't end
But now the episode is over
Going through that horrible condition
Now the numbness has reached its end.

Wait For the Right Time

Namara Lwansa

Standing on the tallest tower,
I think I'm full of power,
Wishing I could fly,
But alas! I can't try.

If I could,
I would,
But I can't,
So I shan't.

Silly me,
To think I could be,
A ruler with a twirl,
Yet I'm just a girl.

Wait for your time,
My friend tells me,
The climb is steep,
The fruits are sweet.

The Good that's in Doom

Namara Lwansa

Peace and Violence, the difference we should distinguish
Conflict, worry ad fear we should extinguish
When a bomb hits boom
Peace is in doom.

Once a bomb hits her
She feels bitter
Peace is feeling gloomy
Peace is in doom.

Never ending continuous violence
will I ever 'hear' silence
Peace is forgotten
Peace is in doom.

Gloom and doom, will peace ever prevail
I hope it will succeed and not fail
The earth sobs
Peace is in doom.

A person I miss

Fautia Mogaeka

When I was born,
I didn't know he was gone,
Until a fateful day,
Oh I wish I could make them pay.

Every step of my life,
Other moments sharp like a knife,
Times he's supposed to be there with me,
But why isn't he?

But no matter where you are,
Even if it's smaller than a jar'
I don't care about other people's hue,
Because I know that I love you.

Love

Fautia Mogaeka

Love is an emotion,
That sets people in motion,
Love is like a treasure,
That we should certainly remember.

Holding others in a warm embrace,
Reminds us of the point of this amazing race,
I'm certain we don't love for fame
Because if we do, then that's really lame

I really don't have much to say,
But I hope my words won't face fade with dismay,
My poem has reached the end,
So put your arms around your dearest friend.

The World's Harmony

Fautia Mogaeka

Peace is something we all dearly require
And it's also something the world needs to aspire
For if we don't, the consequences will be as hot as fire
Peace is the derivation of all harmony.

Without peace we may encounter war
Something that may shake the earth core
And render it bruised and sore
Peace is the derivation of all harmony.

Lack of peace also brings stress
That acts like a blob of motional press
And eliminates the secure embrace
Peace is the derivation of all harmony.

War is like kale
That rots when it's stale
And leaves people pale
So peace be our root of harmony.

Life beyond the Day

Fautia Mogaeka

As the last sun ray fades
And we thank the sun for its aids
New life will be reborn
Thus, I thnk the'll blow a horn.

All that was and is in night time has been revived
But don't ask where it was and how it survived
For that was a secret meant to be concealed
Not something that could just be revealed.

All the heavenly bodies like the moon and stars
Are not easily kept inside empty jars
Their magnificent quality is more than their weights
So don't think you could balance them on lop-sided plates.

People's hearts are filled with incredible zest
When they see these bodies that are part of their crest
Some like bewildering constellations
Although they weren't part of sublimations.

I have at last reached my conclusion
Of something that is not an illusion
But an incredible derivation
That needs our honest congratulation.

Negro Fire

Ian Richard

Waking up from a lynch
I can't believe I survived
I can't even feel the pinch
Of all the rights I was deprived.

My heart is pumping I can't believe
Should I run or help myself and die
Only to find myself next to a snake
Locked in cuff right in jail.

The door closes in front of the face
And everyone I see is white
I can't believe I still have life
But these are the days next to pain.

No way can't they listen even if it rains
I can't believe I survived
Out of the negro fire I derived.

Social

Ian Richard

Boys and girls playing with toys
At the end of the day you get spoiled
Chips and burger come in foiled
"Don't get out of the house," dad says.

All they see is coaches and stairs
They cant get up and say it is not fair
All they do is read lame books
Today or tomorrow they'll become crooks.

Boys and girls try to be social
Watch the news and be informal
Social media was not made for nothing
Instagram, WhatsApp, Flipagram all are made for something.

Try your best to be up-to-date
Not relaxing and being out of date
Social and everything get information
Be international with all preparation.

Evil taking toll

Jasmine Kapya

The time has come,
It's now the beginning of the end,
Everything hanging from its last thread
From destiny to fate.

The fate of destruction created by vices of people,
When the word of God was staple,
The time love was the world's base,
But now conquering all is lies.

As days pass,
Sins grow into faceless beasts
Moving in armies,
Hankering for flesh to devour.

Sin's the only thing man is fond of
Through so many ways
Sins through the touch of hand
Through the work of mind
And through the work of tongue.

People dropping like flies
Ministers becoming corrupt
Leaders engulfed in lies
Why has the world become so daft?

Those who call themselves holy

Are the ones who find themselves falling
Even worshipers take part in the deadly brawls
These are ways evil takes toll.

My iron rose

Jasmine Kapya

The vibrant figure different from all
She an iron rose
She who rises when she falls
No matter the number of blows
To her perseverance out lasts persecutions.

She so exquisite
She full of life
She so deliberate
She who is ready to fight
She a path finder.

Lives a life of wonders
So many unbelievable successes
Who glows in the dark like a star
Changes negative into positive.

A mentor! Yes who taught me to rise to the challenge
You taught me to be me
You taught me never to give up
You taught me never to say never.

Mom, my mentor, my iron rose
My one and only idol
My favorite dancer and singer
My excessive joy bringer.

Graffiti her life

Jasmine Kapya and Glory Fadhili

Take her joy away by lying
Kill her ambition by breaking her heart
Destroy of what's holy in her with sweet touch and words.

Turn what a beautiful temple God built
Into a vandal savage palace
Colouring her outside the lines dull colours
She's trying to escape the truth that she no longer innocent.

Her value scrolled down to a crescent
Her ambition changed into deception
She lost her essence
And made her lose her glorious presence.

He graffitied her life
Like slicing her throat with a knife
She tried to take control of it with all her might
Seems to be her courage faded into plain sight.

She tried to see a beam of light
But her future faded into plain sight
She was in so much fright
Her day turned into a spooky night.

Friendship

Namara and Davynn

We met a long time ago,
When we met it was all hatred
The hate wasn't fated,
It's like our friendship was always destined.

As time went by,
I cannot lie,
We enjoyed each other's company,
Together we are a perfect harmony.

We realized we are a perfect match,
Like the way a hen sees her chick hatch,
We make each other glad,
When we are together we are never sad.

Now we have a strong bond,
Of each other we are really fond,
Together we are Davynn and Namara,
We sparkle like a diamond tiara.

My Companion

Namara Lwansa

She's been with me through thick and thin,
Loves me when I lose or win,
Brought joy when I was sick,
Took care of me when I was weak.

You loved me through sickness or health,
Assisted me during poverty or wealth,
Took in my bad and my good,
And you gave me food.

I look up to you,
The things you do,
My love for you will never end,
Cause I love the time we often spend.

She is my mother,
I love her unlike any other,
Delicious as a slice of pizza,
Her name is Akiza.

My Sister: Chanda

Namara Lwansa

Who is this dear?
Whose name I often hear,
She is as playful as a kitten,
As soft as a mitten.

This 'dear' is sometimes rough,
Almost always tough,
A hard nut to crack,
When she makes a decision no turning back.

We sometimes fight,
I know it's not right,
We love each other,
For we have the same mother.

In conclusion, I love my sister,
We come from the same mister,
She is sometimes as friendly as a panda.
She is my sister named Chanda!

Me

Namara Lwansa

I am not that complicated;
Let me explain,
Let's say I'm dedicated,
In laughter or in pain.

I'm smart,
Some may say,
I have an understanding heart,
I'm kind of special in my own way.

I went through open heart surgery,
Dreadful moment for my parents –
But I survived!
By the Grace of God I survived,
Now I'm here enjoying life.

If you make me angry,
I will make you weary,
I have a sound mind,
And when I seek, I find.
That's me.

I Had a Friend

Princessia Mrema

I had a friend who was nice and wonderful
She was close and like a sister to me
I thought she would be mine and with me
I thought I had a friend who was close to me.

I thought she was mine and could be my bestie
But I thought wrong and she left me sobbing
My tears for her will be forever and close to me
I had a friend who was close to me.

All my life I'll remember the selfies
The things will be forever with me
I love her so much I wish she was with me
I had a friend who was close to me.

A Friend

Ireney Ngayama

Everybody wants to find out
Who they are for real
Looking for a way
To show how I feel.

I aim to turn it up
So don't you turn me down
For when we get together
We go a rocking sound.

No need to follow in
Somebody else's steps
We make our own moves
I think you know the rest.

A melody needs harmony
You have shown me
What a friend can be.

Education

Farida Yahya

Education is something that a person must get
Very important to a child even an adult
Education is the mighty doorway
It is one mighty sunray.

Education is the key to my future
If I don't get education
I won't be who I really want to be
For real education unlocks success.

If you are in school
Don't disrespect the teachers
Workers or even drivers
Respect mirrors education gained.

If you don't have education
Dreams will falter
Steps will slip
And the sun will set at noon.

The Importance of a Mother

Salhia Mchatta

First I was a cell
Then a tissue
After days passed I was an organ
And now I am a kid
Without a mother I cannot live.

She took care of me
She fed me all the milk
She cleared all my poop
Without a mother I cannot live.

I disturbed her at night
But she was patient
She calmed me down
To get my sleep
Without a mother I cannot live.

And now it's my duty
To take care of her
I'll do the dishes and laundry
Without my mother I cannot live.

Peace

Nainkwa Mbati

Peace! What are you?
How do you work?
What do you work on?
Do you go and come back?

How do you make people one again?
How do you make people happy?
How do you make a country develop?
Peace! What are you?

Now I know
You make a country develop
If there is no violence
If there is no war
Peace! You are a very good friend.

You make the country develop
You make people make first class airplanes
You make pupils know technology better than their parents
You are the centre of all.

Life

Chelsea Ilumba

Life is full of ups and downs
Life is the most valuable gift
But people take it for granted
I don't know why.

Life on earth is a mad rush
The price is paid not in cash
But why? I don't understand
Why is this taking place?

Life flows as you guide it
It flows either fast or slow
It purely depends on the glow
Of that internal smouldering ember.

A Mother

Janiyah Abbas

Who is a mother?
I sit myself and wonder
Who has the answer
To my question?
If I get my answer

I will thank God for everything
Oh what a pain if I don't get my answer
Who is a mother? I need to get my answer.

My mother will create my future
My mother will make me a winner
My mother is everything to me
What a wonderful mother.

I love you mother.

Life and Death

Angel Mgaya

Once you hear life and death
A tremor of fear comes to your face
Your mind revolves and heart beats fast
Like a leopard running fast after prey he can't catch.

They say it's invisible but comes fast
Once you get out you must come back
You can be full of joy when you come out
But full of sorrow when you go back.

Life is full of love, hate, passion and betrayal
But death chases emotions that can hold your heartbeat
It is a feeling that you can taste in a second
Just briefly then you fly away.

A Farewell Outpouring

Jasmine Kapya

My reign of power is over,
It's just like a farewell forever,
I used to think that my position was a fantasy;
When I first stepped in,
My whole world change into an unimaginable galaxy,
But now I'm leaving my legacy.

To me, it doesn't matter whether I've left the best,
All that has been thrown to me was a challenging test,
A lot of people said I was powerless,
But I proved to them that I was fearless.

I believe that my team was more victorious.
Their work was not vapid
Their care so elevated
Teachers have called us laudable
They made us noticeable.

I poured all my heart in my work
Even though some wanted to stab me with pitch forks
It has been five good years
Now, I face the world without fear
The extravagant feeling I have seeing this
Blinds me with tears.

The tiny forces achieved great results
We didn't watch the clock only

We kept on going.

I have left others the best
This is only my first step
I wore my title proudly on my chest
I hope all of you are impressed
Now my life's full of zest
For I have passed the test.

Thank you teachers
Thank you pupils
I'll savor all the wild times and thrills
I'll never forget all your wonderful features.

Cold Water

Ian Richard, Irene, Jonathan, Doreen

With your soothing touch I shiver
Like a feeling I get when sweat runs down my spine
Emotionless feeling broad like a river
I can explain when my nerves freeze inside.

Hailstones dropping from the sky
All doors closed from up to down
Every road you see is filled with snowy miles
No one in the playground I end up with a frown.

With such feelings of anger
Its origin stays unknown forever
I just wish it were summer
Just mid June back in Tanzania.

Winter to sunshine you wish
Feeling cold like a box ice
Like a dark angel striking me with lightning
Like a warning through my soul
Feeling cold through my veins
Colder till it makes my bloodstain.
It is neither hot nor warm
And tonsillitis it forms
It doesn't just visit like a norm
Mostly aggressive at the time of a storm.

Warming up myself to get a nap

Only to find myself in a trap
Being lowered in a hole
Trying to save myself on tip toe.

Till I'm plunged inside with a blop
I can't stop shivering without a hop
As I grind my teeth like a wood and saw
Just like its tiny drop is a shock.

Cold water is not a joke
I'm telling all people who peek and poke
Cold water is like smoke
It will make you shed tears even before you know it.

My Imagination in a Book

Fautia Mogaeka

As I open the book,
 Not caring about the look,
Ready to be engulfed,
In a world full of wonder.

As I read the first line,
The picture in my mind is divine,
I forget the world around me,
Oh, the images I see!

Funny people, tall and short,
Riding on the back of a horse,
People playing tag on the shore,
Others building sandy forts.

On and on I read,
Other images leaving me bewildered,
And suddenly I am in the end,
I sit back with a beam,
And Alas! I disappear from my dream.

Night Time

Henry Thomas

The time has come,
For every human to go to bed,
Switch off the light,
And go to sleep.

Relax your brain,
Relax your body,
And let the tiredness go away,
Have good dreams while you are asleep.

Pray to God before sleeping,
Pray so that he can protect you,
And protect other people,
Sleep well, stay safe.

Stepping In

Ian Richard

My heart stops beating,
As I get a strange feeling,
My feet start shaking,
And I can't imagine stepping in.

I've heard all the spoilers,
The fear I had was still boiling,
My mind went crazier,
I felt like I was in a crater.

I thought it was so scary,
Teachers faces were always gloomy,
I thought it would always end up bloody,
With everything all blurry.

But I stepped in so courageous,
And nothing was contagious,
And the spoilers were just rumors,
I'm now finding it fabulous.

I'm now going to finish with no grudges to hold,
I'll remember all moments just like a scroll to fold,
The memories will remain alive
Till I grow white and old.

This Is What It Means To Be a Child

Glory Fadhili

A child, what minor a word,
So complex yet so simple,
Most grow wings and fly like birds,
Because they know what it means to be a child.

Guessing and asking so many questions,
Trying to answer and listening to suggestions,
Stretching and striding to reach for success,
This is what it means to be a child.

Just because you're a child,
Doesn't mean your opinions can't be heard,
Speak, protest and shout loud,
For this is what It means to be a child.

Use these privileges to do what's right,
Be innocent, obedient and right,
For your well wishers won't be lenient,
For this is what it means to be a child.

P

My Love for Reading

Shiloh Kiluwasha

Do you know a book has a hook?
Well let's see and have a look;
When I flip the pages,
I can read for ages,
My eyes glued to the shifting words,
That line the street of ideas.

I look at them like fools,
For I think reading is cool,
And the words I see,
Are what I seek,
Some people say I'm a nerd,
Books are my chosen companions.

And the feeling of getting lost in a book,
Is like someone pulling you with a hook,
And there is no turning back,
Because you're on the right track –
And that is my feeling when i get lost in a book.

A School Experience

Mercy-Anna Kijazi

Early in the morning I wake up,
Go for morning preps,
Feeling too lazy to do so,
What a hard experience!

I tried,
I trusted,
I vowed never to give up but,
What a hard experience!

I feel sloppy and complain,
And ask myself 'What's the big deal?'
An answer is not readily available.

I feel a scare,
And I flare,
Will I get there?
My brow feels hot;
But my heart weakly shouts:
 "I'll never give up."

P

Love

Steven Kidindima

Love is good ,
Love is life,
Love is precious,
Love starts in you,

Love is gracious ,
It comes from the bottom of the heart,
It brings kindness to people,
Love starts in you.

Love shows the right direction,
It brings peace and unity,
Love is godliness,
Love starts in you.

Love taking toll

Jasmine Kapya

Love is a feeling so warm,
Anytime hate thunders in like a storm,
No one is safe from the hideous form,
That's why love takes all when its your norm.

The bond in love is unbreakable,
And it is unshakable,
Compare love and hate obviously love is more capable,
That's why love takes all in the humble,

With love you shall never crumble,
Believe in it and it shall believe in you,
Don't doubt or else you'll stumble,
But love takes toll in very few.

Love your enemies, the good books say,
With promise of abundant joy,
If you keep in your heart, your smile will never fade,
Let's hold hands and have a blast today.

Night fall

Jasmine Kapya.

It's dark and you feel sleepy,
Probably you're used to it but it's kind of creepy,
The time dream star wanders,
From everywhere to every yonder.

When night fall comes,
Darkness is awakened,
Don't worry the sun shines at dawn,
The morning brightness is still fated.

You wake up suddenly,
You're shaken abruptly,
While the ferocious creatures crawl
You'll definitely know it's nightfall.

The Light
Doreen Mosha

I am the natural satellite,
I shine bright from the sky,
I look down on everything ,
I think of the light I bring.

I am everything in the world,
Without me the world is dark,
I give vitamin D,
And help in photosynthesis.

I am the total of all these conditions,
I describe the weather of the day,
I rise in the morning and shine,
I set in the evening, smiling,
 I am the Sun.

In the Dark

Davynn Faraja, Grace, Kayden, Nicole, Vida

I was in left in the dark,
Then suddenly I heard a bark,
I thought I would see a spark,
But it was bad luck.
I stared at the window,
I felt frightened,
My eyes fell in and my teeth fell out,
My fingers felt clammy.

It is a terrible feeling,
That people may think of killing,
It is a feeling that is unbearable,
That would never be comparable.

I feel a tremble,
Like everything is about to rumble,
And my world is about to crumble,
Slipping from tumble to tumble.

It makes my heart pump fast,
Dashing the one minute past,
The definite angelic presence,
Of all imaginable decency.

I was trembling in fear,
Suddenly I felt a tear,
I thought I was torn apart,
But I was brave and alert.

Fear an empty word,
Which sounds so absurd,
To some it is a fad,
So generously offered.

I Am

Christina Mlay

I am white,
I come from the clouds in the rain,
Many people see me,
Who am I?

I am the terror,
Of the sticky smile,
I travel faster than my friend,
A discreet fiend,
 I am lightning.

The Weather in Me

Namara Lwansa

I am the ray of light,
I can easily calm a fright,
I wake those feeling sleepy,
I am friendly not creepy.
I bring joy to the joyless,
I bring care to the careless,
Let the darkness disappear,
For, I'm here.

I bring love to those hated,
My sentence has been stated,
I bring happiness to pass the time,
Teach troublemakers not to commit crime,
I am a ray of sunshine!

Night Time

Namara Lwansa

As I lie here,
Feeling the endless fear,
Of being woken from slumber,
And being shocked by thunder.

Lying on my bed paranoid,
As if I'm trapped internally in a void,
Don't wake me up I say,
I am resting, don't take it away.

The time has come,
I hear a hum,
Who is it?
It's my mum.

That's my night time,
Not as sour as lime,
The feeling can be special,
It makes me feel celestial.

Who am I?

Joanne Mteteri

I am the goddess of the land,
I am the light in the darkness,
I am the heat of the cold,
Who am I?
I am the way for the blind,
I am the centre of the galaxy,
I am the first thing you see in a day,
I am sunshine.

If my dog could Talk

Nathaniel Ondigo

If my dog could talk, humans would be quiet,
As long as it barks, humans do talk,
And when it barks, thunders whisper,
What a wonder it would be, if my dog could talk.

Dogs bark when in danger, humans talk so aimlessly,
And when it plays with you, it is a friend so true,
What a wonder it would be, if my dog could talk.

Street dogs face untold heartaches,
Humans beat them with forks, what a shock!
Dogs don't eat with forks, pelt them with the same,
What a wonder it would be, if my dog could talk.

Dogs don't speak words, they show actions,
They understand both love and hate,
Is it a case of coloured fate?
What a wonder it would be, if my dog could talk.

Night Time
Vida Frank Mapunda

A time that it is dark,
When dogs usually bark,
While going to the park,
What a scary night time.

A time that you sleep tight,
Such a fitting flight,
The moon shows a bright darkness,
As time goes into blindness.

A time that you lie down looking at the sky,
Feeling that you are on the sty,
The heart bottles a cry,
What a struggling try.

A time when a bat flits,
And an owl loudly hoots,
A time that the windows shatter,
Does all this really matter?

The Grade Seven Experience

Nicole Kamando

It is a very hard time,
And things are sour like limes,
I wished I had dimes,
To overcome the grade seven experience.

I missed 6th grade,
When life was home made,
And ideas I used to trade,
These times are now fade.
I want to achieve my dreams,
Because grade seven is an A team,
And I shall shine like a light beam,
While eating some ice-cream.

I learnt that regret will never turn a clock,
Because the clock keeps going tick-tock,
Grade seven to me is school of rock,
I love this experience.

Mothers in the World

Davynn Faraja

Oh! What a wonderful word,
Mothers are very intelligent,
They help us in every matter,
No mothers, no world.

Mothers are very intelligent,
Without your mum you wouldn't exist,
So we should all desist,
From despising our mothers.

And it is said,
In the shadows of a successful man,
There's a brilliant woman,
So no mothers, no world.

My Life
Davynn Faraja and Jasmine Kapya

I live a life of gold,
But my story has never been told,
As you continue reading it will start to unfold,
Right out of its beautiful mould.

I always had a hard life,
But I survived,
It was a long drive,
But I always had my humble thrive.

At times I may stumble,
But no one cares so just stay humble,
Your haters will always want you to crumble,
Just keep yourself away from trouble.

Time is never on your side,
Anytime you can be hit by a high tide,
You may fall and slide,
But learn how to bide.

There are people who will always be proud,
But just keep silent and never make a sound,
Always let your actions speak loud,
To other people you are just another person in the crowd.

I may have had a rough past,
I know my life is never gonna last,

Just enjoy every moment and have a blast,
But keep your time because time flies fast.

I was born in the streets,
But I had people steadying my feet,
Then suddenly they all vanished in a blink,
I didn't know what to do, I couldn't even think.

At times people may break my heart,
But I have to face the situation I have,
No one can discourage me,
And what I have to do is stay calm.

I won't give up on myself,
And nothing matters but my opinion itself,
My struggle in life is my precious wealth,
As I stand with strong health.

This is my story,
I hope it wasn't boring,
And I know I've lived a life of gold,
For I am strong, brave and bold.

A Sad Moment

Sharon Ayittah

I once had a father,
Who was caring and loving,
He always had passion,
For his only daughter.

One day I woke up,
My room was alive,
People's eyes filled with tears,
The mood of the room was only gloom.

I asked what was going on,
But no one seemed to answer,
My heart lurched,
Nerves stood on end.

They started arguing,
On who to tell me the truth
They made a decision,
My mother was chosen.

She started talking,
And I was so afraid,
She said that,
My dad was scheduled to work in America.

I was filled with both joy and sadness,
Hearing that, brought loneliness,

But also brought happiness,
Knowing that my dad got a good job.

After a while,
I looked at my dad,
And he said to me,
Never give up.

God will always be with you,
Keeping you safe all the time,
You can always trust in him,
But do not make him a gold mine.

He then left,
I felt like he had left with my heart,
But I took his advice,
Took care of my mom,
And I thank God for everything.

Slavery
Shiloh Kiluwasha

A system so dark,
As hard as a tree bark
Being tied up with a rope
As their sorry tears drop.

Let's break the chain, that evil has reign
Oh the discrimination, what happened to the nation
People working day and night, without knowing their rights
They look at the sky, thinking they can fly.

Their sorry tears,
They think they will do it for years,
They are afraid to open their ears
To listen to their fears.

By the cruel traders
They invaded us as raiders
Pretending to be leaders
But they are just the haters.

People were working,
Without pay,
And lived out their lives
Without a light ray.

A School It Is

Roselyne Mlingwa, Kuyi, Alvin and Larry

At early morn, an annoying horn,
Stirs me from deep sleep,
At the lawn, off goes the drone,
All the way to school.

A nice environment,
Filled with bloom and bliss,
A peaceful environment,
Ready to birth mighty accomplishments.

It's called a school,
And it's super cool,
Like a mighty pool,
Our fatigue to pull.

High standard teachers,
With knowledge of smart preachers,
Ready to mould us like scriptures,
Oh, what beautiful features!

Wishy-washy, gloomy teachers?
Oh no! Happy creatures,
Hard, solid like stone,
Just like King Kong.

Bob Rich at the gate,
Ready to all update,

With intricacies of this life,
Yes, how to evade life's knife!

Here I start my day,
Ready to make a way,
To all that sways,
As I hit the sun rays.

Embracing Literacy is our motto,
Education is our cool photo,
That we hang in the hallway of fame;
Yes, a cool school it is!

Advice to A Lazy Person

Emmanuel Mkangaa, Sarah, Armstrong and Jessie

Not getting off the sofa
Thinking that nobody will care
Lazy to even comb your hair
Is any of this really fair?

Do something with your life
Train yourself to be fit
Do your best
And forget the rest.

Laziness can make you fat
People will see you as a spoiled brat
Chase you away like a rat
Leave you like a stray cat.

You'll end up hated
With your stomach inflated
Do something now
Or you'll regret it.

An Absentee Father

Gift Siyame, Rahma, Ethan and Melvin

Father's footsteps are heard for the first time in days,
Mother gets up and holds a spade,
"Open the door," father yells,
Mom tells me to be still.

Morning comes and we're all alone again,
Mom's bruised yet flashes a smile my way,
I see her holding back tears but I'm not that strong,
So I run upstairs and cry all day long.

I sleep without a proper meal,
I don't get it, what's his deal?
Why did he marry my mother?
Did he really have to become my father?

I give up on him,
For he'll only come back in my dreams,
I have to start fending for the family,
I'm only five, why did he do this to me?

Oh father,
What have you done to mother and I?
You've left us all alone,
To fight life's battles on our own.

This is so unfair,
I dare say this so-called father is a bag of air,

I pray I don't grow up to be him,
From today this father is no more to me.

Stressed Out

Alvin Jamie

Fear with frustration
Has no explanation
With no sense of reaction
Filled with hesitation.

Every day a new burden to carry
Every day a loud yell to hurry
Unfair treatment to human kind
That births a strayed mind.

Awkwardness fills the air
Everyone starts to stare
Waiting for you to make a mistake
Waiting…waiting for a swooping retake.

Trying so hard to be perfect
While everyone says you are worthless
Discouraging you second after second
Killing you slowly to the last crumb.

Our Parents

Brian Moses

Parents are our family,
They raise us well,
They also give us a name.

If we love our parents,
We love our family.
That is God's word.

God knows us all,
Even before our birth,
Because he knows our parents.

Why should we cry,
While our parents love us,
We should thank God for them.

If it weren't for the them,
If they didn't raise us,
What would become of the family?

Parents are the heads of the family tree,
Because they lead the family,
In the right direction.

When our parents die,
We cry for them,
That shows that we love them so much.

Don't worry about your parents,
If they're righteous in God's eye
For they shall be with God.

When we know this,
God says "Don't worry",
Our parents are in our hearts.

When our parents treat us well,
That parent is blessed,
And so is the family.

We should not take them for granted
And the care they give us,
Is a blessing to future generations.

Thank you God for my parents,
Now you reader and listener,
It is your turn to thank God for your parents.

May God's name be praised.

My Mother

Sharon Ayittah

She is a beautiful woman
The most patient lady I know;
She gave birth to me
Even though it was a lot of pain
Mother, what a wonderful lady you are!

She has good cooking skills
She always loves us
She usually gives good advice
Mother, what a wonderful lady you are!

She is a kind lady
She is always comforting
She is a good wife to my dad
Mother, what a wonderful lady you are!

She knows how to drive the car of life
She knows how to heal
The wounds of the heart
She is a wonder woman,
Mother, what a wonderful lady you are!

The Race

Davin Abrahamsson

This was the biggest race
Time to show what I did embrace
It was time to get out of the cocoon
And avoid making myself swell.

Time to take a huge flight
To hide from stifling fright;
In order to escape this scary plight
I have to do this with all my might.

It's time to climb up this hill
Even if it means getting very ill
I will not hide
I will take the day with a ride.

For I will not hide
I will stick with my side
I won't walk a stride
If I lose, I'll know I tried.

I will be the guy
Who's faster than a fly
This time I'll not cry
As I win the ultimate race.

Hypocrites
Davin Abrahamsson

People who act like friends,
Always make your life bend,
When offended you will know,
Even if you're born in the same realm.

At times you will call them super cool,
When you're not with them they call you a fool,
You find these people at school,
I hate hypocritical fools.

Hypocrites are so wrong,
Even though they may be strong,
And pull a mighty throng,
To this razor-edged prong.

Hypocrites are so bad,
They sometimes make you sad,
They sometimes make you mad,
Even if you're just a jolly lad.

My Parents
Doreen Mosha

I love my parents,
They are my guardians,
They are my purpose,
They are my loved ones.

They are my everything,
Never wanting to see me suffering,
Always caring,
They are my loved ones.

Angry, they are not
Laziness is not their sport,
Happiness is their thing,
For they are my loved ones.

They are always tough and serious,
Not the ones to be so mysterious,
Their words are very precious,
For their love is very gracious.

Save a Soul

Emmanuel Mkangaa

Please, save a soul,
Before I die in a big hole,
Or get eaten by a big mole,
Yes, eaten in a big bowl,
Or get my head cracked on a wall.

Please, save a soul,
For if I don't reach my own big goal,
I will die in a pit of coal,
And I will not get my important call,
I will have a huge fall.

Please, save a soul,
Or I'll die before my day,
Right in a pit of hay,
Or if a guy says "hey" to me,
He's going to have to pay the fee.

Please, save a soul,
Before I'm alone,
Or I lose my phone,
In a tub of ice cone,
Right in front of my clone.

Give me some help
Before I make a loud yelp
If you don't, I'll die,

2PPP 2 g e P

P

And become an angel and fly,
So just help me with a pie.
Oh, please save a soul,
Please save us All!

Falling Ain't Failing

Maureen Geoffrey, Calvin, Anitha and Tracey

Ever passed through a taxing time
So tedious and devastating
Goosebumps, on every part of your skin appear
Afraid of what tomorrow brings.

Feeling confident and energetic
Knowing you can always ace it
Sleeping soundly and happily
Awaking with a confident smile.

Take a seat
A paper of hostility
God knows who made it
A scream, a shout.

Results arrive
Looking at them with awe
"Why?" you ask,
"Failure! That's what it is."

People sometimes fail in their lives
Everyone in life slips sometimes
But if you work hard you can succeed
And erase sorrow and sadness.

Yes, failure is everyone's pathway
We all know how it feels

Crying when everyone else is laughing
Such a devastating feeling.

Even the Chinese can fail in life
Despite their success they can fail once or twice
Failing brings inspiration
And loads of wet motivation.

Just Do It
Francis Albert

In life there are problems,
It's our work to solve them,
And defeat them,
My advice to you is 'just do it'.

There is always an inspiration,
But you just have to look for it,
Always find it well without manipulation,
My advice to you is 'just do it'.

In life there are hard times,
They're always hard and bitter as limes,
They are always sad just likefrench mimes,
My advice to you is 'just do it'.

In life, treasure needs to be found,
Not just picked off the ground,
Definitely not to be kicked around,
My advice to you is 'just do it'.

Life isn't as hard as you think,
And it doesn't really stink,
But you just got to smile and wink,
My advice to you is 'just do it!'

The Nairobi Experience

Sharon Ayittah

It was a Saturday afternoon
I was at the airport
Alighting from the Kenya airways plane
Into a place filled with surprises
Into a city of wonders.
In this country called Kenya
There is a city named Nairobi
A city filled with sckyscrappers
All glittering in the sun
What a city!
It's nice to be in a tall building
Where you can see the blinking lights
The view is very beautiful
I wish I had it all
What an experience!
I visited the national park,
It was the Nirobi National Park
It has wonderful animals
And such pristine surroundings.
Nairobi has low temperature
It is one of its good features
I wish this were my second home
But I guess I'll just be a tourist.
There are churches too
Which are filled with God-fearing people
At least I get to be a temporary member

Truly a time to remember
What an experience!
There are schools too
I wish I could join them
But I guess that's just a dream
What an experience!
I really want to live there
But my home is Tanzania
It was truly exciting to be there
But I have to go back home.

Life Expression
Gift Siyame

There are different expressions in life,
Happiness and sadness are some,
For a second you're happy then sad,
Why, why is life like this?

In school we have friends and studies,
Yet we have best friends and enemies,
And again we have winners and losers,
Why, why is life like this?

When in school be careful,
You might win and lose at the same time,
You win you're happy, you lose you're sad,
Why, why is life like this?

Tell you about school?
It is a place where you and I learn,
It is a place of reality,
Why, why is life like this?

Talk about friends and enemies,
Your best friends are your enemies,
Look into the eye and find out,
Why, why is life like this?

Competition is always there,
You might win or lose you just don't know,

If you win and they lose they become jealous of you,
Why, why is life like this?

The moment you win twice or more,
They turn away for good,
Instead they end up being fake friends,
Why, why is life like this?

The Man

Gift Siyame

There is a man
Who teaches until you understand
Even if you're an empty can
You'll be charged until you run
Which has been so much fun.

His teaching is amazing
And so is his poetry
You'll like it when he recites them
Why not follow them?
If you can, make it a game.

His poems inspire me a lot
And his teachings get me inside a boat
This is greater than all I've ever bought
For once I had thought
My conclusion had been made.

With some finishing touches I can say
This good man takes you out of the dark
Brings you back to the light
He is very kindhearted and ambitious
What an experience it's been.

Temptations and Sins

Ian Richard

Temptations and sins are,
The world's basic possessions,
That surrounds this fateful sphere
Of temptations and sins.

Temptations pull emotions,
Those erotic commotions;
Temptations are crawling,
Inside people's bodies,
Temptations and sins.

Walking along the road,
By the bush beside the road,
She hears a whisper with a crooked voice,
Temptations pull her beside the bush,
And dragged, she is, into the bush,
Whatever happens is never to be revealed.

The world is not holy,
Churches are falling, failing…
Pastors are lying,
Money is the father of,
Temptations and sin.

People die in the bush,
The bush of sin and temptations,
Premarital sex crowns its activity

HIV greets you on the road of death,
Sins fry you on temptations' pan,
Which is, to be honest, zero percent fun.

Under the Same Sky

Janet Kateti

We all know it,
We all conquer it,
We all live under it,
Everyone is under the same sky.

Both city and countryside,
Rich and poor,
Some have agoraphobia,
Everyone is under the same sky.

The prisoners and the free,
Take not life for granted,
The world is full of vices,
Everyone is under the same sky.

There are agonized cries,
All around the streets,
The rich and the poor howl for recognition,
Just like everyone else under the sky.

People are suffering,
They are hungering for sweet air,
That brings bits of good news,
To everyone under the same sky.

What Conquers All?

Jasmine Kapya

They say time is money,
Others say money is time,
So is money a crime?
What conquers all: money or time?

It is easy for the rich to go through a needle's eye,
Compared to one going to heaven,
Money might be power, but time's never a coward,
What conquers all: money or time?

You might be cool in the future,
In real sense you are a fool,
Fancy cars, new suits are your time's prime pursuits,
What conquers all: money or time?

You might rightly wonder,
If you're wise you will not despise,
Time is power, money is a coward,
What conquers all: money or time?

Life

Joshua Lukumay

Life is a heart or soul
That stays in a hole
And cannot be played
Like a ball.

Days pass by
Like the birds that fly
And it is never dry
For life is the sky.

There is a time you fail
There's a time you feel pain
There's a time you gain
There's a time you wish for no pain.

But having fun and eating a burger
And carrying a soda to work
Is just but a tip
In the big life bus.

Flower

Karren Felix

It is wonderful,
And also colourful,
It turns out amazing,
It is beautiful.

It is spotless,
All the insects are thoughtless,
Whether to touch it or not,
And it is not 'wonderless'.

It is always blooming out in the morning,
And blooming in the evening,
It is not just a thing,
It is above the value of a king.

Without hesitating,
The flower is kidnapping,
The beasts and the kings
It is a real queen of incarnations.

To hell I sentence
The intruders' impudence
I swear to protect my princess
To keep in my precincts.

And enjoy her scents
That's all I wish

Only that there aren't horses
They exist in my instincts.

My flower is my distinction
My excellent divination
The hope of my generation
Because it's without deception.

Full of power of accumulation
The solution to my calculation
In every algebraic equation
Of life distribution
My flower, you are my queen.

Albinos

Kuyi Nanai

From a Greek word it came
Passed on from generation to generation
Father, mother all affected
It cannot be prevented.

White skin, white hair
NO! It is never fair
Contributions, agreements and different terms
It was never caused by a germ.

Hundreds and thousands affected
They never chose it, they never wanted
Cuts, bruises and burns
They can get hurt under the sun.

Please save the affected
Feel sorry for the afflicted
Treat them as your own kindred
Please do and don't mind.

Like us, they have rights
They can walk, run, talk if they might
Please don't pick a fight
Spare them for it is right.

My Little Chipmunks

Laura Kombo

Living with these two people is crazy drama,
They make me go round and round in circles
It is like riding a roller coaster that never ends.

Living with these two people is living with two chipmunks
Their noise is like banging nails into my ears
It is just so annoying.

At the same time,
Living with them is living with two little angels
It has also been a great adventure living with them
Together we share bits of ourselves.

They're fun to be around at times
They maybe chipmunks but they are my little chipmunks
These people are my little brothers – Jason and Jeremiah.

I'll Never Give Up

Lisa Ndobho

I am a child with dreams
Forever I must scream
I have goals to achieve;
I won't change them
No matter how much you persuade me.

Sometimes life is tough
But you must be tougher
Oiling it with laughter
Lifting your dreams farther.

But I will never give up
No matter what comes my way
I will always man up
Because nothing is impossible
The word itself says 'I'm possible'.

I have learned
The best way to predict your future
Is to create it
And the ONLY one to shut your dreams is you
Don't let anyone shut them for you.

People can talk about your dreams
And make them look like negative things
But I don't care
I believe, finally I will get my PhD

And a great doctor I will be;
Listen to your heart
And you will understand.

It's Your Life To Live
Maureen Geoffrey

Life is like a game,
You either win or lose,
If you win, you'll lose,
If you lose, you must win.

Sometimes I'm afraid to be who I am,
But I always remind myself,
That no matter what I do,
It's my life to live.

Sometimes I feel like I've no one by my side,
But that isn't a big deal,
The whole world might be against me,
But it's my life to live.

I have people who pretend to be my friends,
Hypocrites! They are called,
Some want me to fall,
But that's not my goal.

One thing I've learnt is that,
People change like chameleons,

Sometimes the person you'd take a bullet for
Is the one behind the trigger,
Life's that unfair.

But what I know is that,
Real Friends are out there,
And someday I'll meet them,
They're my guardian angels.

Oh yeah! One thing I almost forgot,
When people pretend to be you,
You just tell them one thing:
Honey, I'm me and that's something you'll never be!

Me, Myself and I

Maureen Geoffrey

I was dead asleep,
When I heard noises of people, crying and yelling,
I thought it was a dream,
So I tried to open my eyes wide.

To my surprise there was a person in front of me,
"Go tell them to shut up! I'm trying to sleep!" I yelled,
He just looked at me as if I was running insane,
Little did I know that he had news for me.

I was still lying on my bed,
Molly, you need to know something, he said.
Tell me later, can't you see I'm asleep! I yelled.
He looked straight into my eyes and said:
You really need to know.

I raised my head and looked around me,
My room was filled with people I didn't know,
I got even more confused,
I knew there was something wrong,
I think you should know, came his voice.

Molly, are you ready? he asked,
I am ready, I replied;
Your dad is NO MORE,
So blunt, so sharp, so…
Suddenly a cloud of tears blinded me.

I cried so hard till the tear well run dry,
I felt as if someone had plunged a sword into my heart,
I took a pillow and covered my head with it.
I wept till my head hurt.

I had never had the love of a dad,
I thought I would experience it,
But I guess that's just how life is unfair,
I guess it's just me against the world.

But no!
I have my friends,
They get me and they'll always be there for me,
They make me feel that I am not alone,
I always have a shoulder to lean on,
They are the ones I cherish most.

Iron Woman
Maureen Geoffrey

She's one of the bravest women I know,
Actually she is the first,
A woman with vision,
A woman with anointing.

A woman who has been hit by the biggest storms,
A woman who never gives up,
A woman who never boasts,
She amazes many.

A kind, caring woman,
A woman who is never noticed,
A woman who is special in her own way,
She is the iron woman.

A woman made of the hardest minerals on earth,
Minerals harder than diamond,
She is hard at heart, courageous and diligent,
I know all these might seem unreal,
But it's what I think.

She isn't famous or anything,
She just surprises me,
She's my role model,
She's my one and only – Mother!

Education

Melvin Kimario

Education is full of joy,
Filled with fantasy,
It is a cause for happiness,
And smiles on everyone's face.

It brings knowledge and intellectual thoughts,
To bring grace and desire of studying,
Nothing can move without knowledge,
Without education, you're nothing.

It is the key to life,
And the opening to success,
If you don't have it, your mind becomes useless,
You use it like a button and just press.

Education has insidious waves,
That try to stop you,
But never lose hope,
Go on strong and you will succeed,

It is needed in life,
With it nobody will kill you,
Nobody will get hurt in a fight,
For it is a way so right.

Teachers

Melvin Kivugo

They paint pupils' minds
And guide their thoughts;
They share their achievements
And clear their faults.

They do inspire a love
For knowledge and truth
And light the path
Which leads our youth.

For the dawn of each poet
Each philosopher and king
Begins with a teacher
And the knowledge they bring.

P

Fear

Neema Bishota

A good morning,
With great meaning,
But with lots of fear,
Oh! What is this fear?

Given a paper in my hand,
Thinking that it's hard,
With heaviness in my head,
Trying to predict and proceed,
Oh! What is this fear?

Questioning myself so quietly,
And do the calculations so fast,
Praying to GOD to answer me carefully,
A headache hits me mercilessly,
Oh! What is this fear?

I speak to myself and meditate
So that I do not skip facts
In order to manage and equip,
My life with strength
Oh! What is this fear?

Phew! The fear is no more,
It's time to make the highest score,
To move from the bottom to centre,
And for us to be better,

So that fear will never enter.

Street Children
Precious Mwageni

Street children are isolated, and also humiliated,
They are extremely despised, and overly tortured,
They pray all day and night, not to be in that case,
Who should be blamed for this situation?

The parents run from the blame, thinking what to say,
It is really a big shame to their parents,
They search for their aim; they seem to be lame,
Who should be blamed for this situation?

Every time they smile, their hearts seems to be in a pile,
They seem to lie, when they are about to die,
They always inspire, the people of desire,
Who should be blamed for this situation?

They work like slaves in castles,
With nothing to call their own
They hardly eat nor look neat,
Who should be blamed for this situation?

Live Your Life

Rahma Elly

The world isn't there forever,
It can always end whenever,
So for the time you have on this earth,
Make every moment worth a life!

Everything in this world happens for a reason,
So if you don't get what you want this season,
Or maybe you get caught up in treason,
Don't give yourself a false final decision.

Live life to the fullest,
You never know when you can lose it,
For these roads on earth can take us to places,
That can start something new for all the races.

In life you will always have a fear,
Sometimes it can make you shed a tear,
But when you overcome it, there will be a cheer,
Coming from everyone near.

If you have an idea, use it,
Quick before you lose it,
For one man can change the world,
And renew everything with just a word!

What Is True Beauty?

Roselyne Mlingwa

Every day I look into a mirror,
Taking hours to perfect thelook,
Examining my very self, from mirror to mirror,
Thinking of what others will say,
Taking a step back from self-confidence.

What is true beauty? Is it hiding behind makeup?
Or putting on the perfect outfit, the perfect dress,
Hiding the real you, putting on lipstick and foundation
Curious what others will say of your look.

As I walk towards the east,
I see women struggling for theperfect outfit,
As I look to the west,
Women are being criticized accordingto their look,
Even the beloved of their friends, look down upon them,
As if that's not enough, even their husbands judge them.

All beauty is within you, not the outside appearance,
Even if you fill yourself with makeup,
Or go to the extent ofplastic surgery,
You can never change who you are, no one ever can,
Never listen to people's judgment,
Turn a deaf ear to their voicings.

To all readers, women and children,
Give me your ears, listen to my words,

Beauty is on the inside, not the outside,
You're not your outside appearance
Appreciate who you really are.

And you so called friends, you so called husbands,
Support the ones you love, give the strength to fight,
Don't judge or criticize them, love them always,
Appreciate them for they might not be with you tomorrow.

Who Am I?

Shiloh Kiluwasha

I am all alone in the house where I came from
Should I cry?
Or should I lie.

I am a girl in the shower
A girl full of power
Is my heart made of gold?
Or is it made of coal?

When I go to school
Should I be cool
Or should I be a fool
When I lose my shoe.

Am I a slave
Working to my grave?
Am I a lover
Or am I hater?
Should I wonder
Or should I howl
Tell me: Who am I?

God Will Make A Way

Suzelle Tesha

You might think you are going through tough times
Maybe tougher than you thought
And you sit there crying day after day
Not knowing who to lean on.

No one might seem to understand you
Some might say you were not born to shine
Which to many is just fine
You sit and cry all day.

At times you pass through devastating times
You feel like giving up
Your heart is dampened and torn
As everybody mocks you.

In the grand scheme of things
There is a father who cares for you
One you can trust to have your back
He will never forsake nor neglect you.

Through the darkest of times he is ever present
He will make a way through thick and thin
When you fall He will take you back to your feet
He is always there as He solemnly promised.

Colours

Virginia Augustine

Stop for a minute and think about this
Imagine the world without these
Pink, purple, yellow and blue
Without these colours there wouldn't be a clue.

Imagine everything grey,
It would be like eating hay
Yes there's a way
That all these colours say.

Think about those butterflies,
And those beautiful birds
All those children screaming with joy,
Leaving behind all their toys.

So colours are important,
Because they shine so bright,
You could even get a fright,
And be thankful for what is right.

Without colours it would be sick,
Nothing in the whole world would flick,
But with colours you just smile and wink,
Because when you look at them you just think.

So colours are really cool,
We all learned them at school,

Anyone who hates them is a fool,
And that's why I give this poem to you.

Responsibility
Benedict Lyimo

It is one of the best virtues
A combination of response and ability
Without it, life is ruined
Without it, existence is soiled.

It needs skill and agility
Maturity is an important ingredient
In the recipe of responsible living
Whose full meal is taken with relish.

It is precious and intangible
Though its results are visible,
It works under the covers
Building a wholesome individual.

With responsibility comes great power
And immense ability to respond well
When duty comes calling
As it often does.

Responsibility is not a matter of age
It comes embraced in mighty wage

It may not be easy to just engage
Please do get into its laborious cage.

Life and Death

Brian Moses

Death takes the finish,
It falls like drops of varnish,
It comes from the unknown benefit,
Which comes to the taken finite.

Life strikes death itself,
Which lives in its own self,
But its day takes its will,
To take its word and kill.

If it is accommodated fast,
It should be destroyed first,
It can be seized with care,
If the interruption can't dare.

Life is the king of energy,
That takes unlimited tragedy,
When forced to live the day,
It can't have its role to play.

Life and death fall apart,
That one should be torn apart,

They accept only the survivors,
They accept only the strivers.

South Korea

Gift Siyame

South Korea, South Korea,
Beautiful and peaceful country,
Filled with handsome men and beautiful women,
South Korea... What a country!

Good beyond measure,
World of heaven filled with angels,
Cool and fresh air abounds,
South Korea... What a country!

Filled with features, beautiful creatures,
Demigods, gods, legends, actors and actresses,
Ever there never to leave you alone,
South Korea...What a country!

Awesome movies grace its airwaves,
The zoos abound with different creatures,
Ever clean and never dirty,
South Korea... What a country!

Guardian angels beautiful as ever,
Living wonders miraculous actions,

Forever living as legends of the country,
South Korea... What a country!

Golden rainbows of living colours,
Flashes of lightning roars of thunder,
Filled with wonders awesome wonders,
At the mention of the name South Korea!

One Child Can Change the World

Gracious Wasley

Stuck in a world where everyone's cruel,
Everything around you sounds devastating,
You try to speak up but no one seems to care,
Bloodshed, bullet stains, corpses everywhere.

Trying to be heard,
But everyone's ears are closed,
Everyone's devastated,
They have no idea of what's coming.

You try to speak up,
But everyone thinks you're useless,
Why? You ask,
Because you're a child.

Can't a child speak?
Isn't he like everyone else?
Can't he share ideas?
What's so wrong about that?

They ignore children,
And children complain,
Adults do idle talk,
Can't we think?

Children complaining,
That they can talk but no one cares,

And not knowing that a child can be,
Someone they all wished to be!

Poverty

Imam Mogaeka

Poverty, a very strange disease
An illness that brings restlessness
A disease caused by laziness
A disease that needs people's awareness.

Poverty, a troubling situation
That is sometimes caused by lack of education
It also brings a lot of nuisance
That is birthed by negligence.

Poverty, a situation that brings sympathy
That needs people's great empathy
It also brings lots of agony
And dismay crowns its cake.

Poverty is a very cruel situation
That is also caused by poor decisions
Poverty is awful
And can also be very dreadful.

Listeners, please take this into consideration
For this matter needs a lot of concentration

It is our obligation to stop poverty
And get rid of horrible tragedy.

Peace

Nancy Mushi

We teach more hate than love
Yet we question where love is
God gave us this earth out of love
Why do we hate each other?
To live is to love, why are we killing one another?
Let's promote peace because we need each other.

Love is the answer for the world's problems
Because it conquers all
People think fighting will make things right
But trust me, it worsens it
All that we have been fighting for all days and nights
Let's promote peace because we need each other.

A World without peace is a world of fear
Nothing will work, just war, chaos and tears
What pains me are the victims, innocent children
Women and the disabled who can't fight run or catch a spear
Let's promote peace because we need each other.

I wish to see a world where we lived in peace and harmony
People from different cultural backgrounds, race, religion
And economic status enjoying all together

It is possible and it starts with you.
With God on our side this world is a better place
Let's promote peace because we need each other.

A Poem for Peace

Nicole Kamando

Peace is a treasure,
Something very hard to measure,
With peace you live in pleasure,
Not only pleasure but also leisure,
Peace makes you pure,
But it shouldn't have a cure.

With peace, we can make the world a better place,
A world with peace has a pure face,
Peace will destroy the bad human race,
Along with the bad tempting shoe lace,
Peace will leave no trace,
Of any bad case.

Peace is never found in a book,
Inside your heart is where you have to look,
Peace traps the bad guys on a hook,
By eating pizza made by a cook,
And never calls them a crook,
The bad guys apologize for what they took.

Peace comes from your heart,
It never brings us apart,
It's a priceless work of art,

Feeling so good you can't smell a goat's fart,
Brings me a mood of shopping in a mart,
Peace makes you do your part.

I really don't have much to say,
May peace shine like a light ray,
And peace will be with us everyday,
Peace never fills us with dismay,
Peace makes us enjoy our day,
It is the encompassing dawn we seek.

Peace

Davynn Faraja

Oh! Peace,
You are everything to me,
You are a valuable thing,
Peace! Peace! You're my wish.

Oh! Peace,
With you I'm not sad,
You make me glad,
Peace! Peace! You're my wish.

Oh! Peace,
You are a bling,
You make me sing,
Peace! Peace! You're my wish.

Oh! Peace,
On you, we cling,
Because joy you bring,
Peace! Peace! You're my wish.

Oh! Peace,
You're my saviour,
You're a sweet smelling savour
Peace! Peace! You're my wish.

People to the World

Ian Cyiza Richard

A word that is self explanatory,
With love not to be tested in a laboratory
And a heart that is keen and well written,
A word that can dry lips when it's spoken.

It is necessary to have it or you'll be broken,
Like a glass from the sky shattered in droplets,
With it I wonder in confidence,
And love conquers with perseverance.

Once a place faces its disappearance,
It will be like a vacuum,
Chaos here, chaos there,
Blown up houses and noise everywhere.

Causing havoc and no tear gas like a surprise,
Protesting for reasons and plenty wars to declare,
Terrorists and criminals all turn out like a surprise,
Robbers with pimples all with guns to advertise.

A day cannot end without a fight,
Nor can it end without a hijacked flight,
Boom and bam through the streets,
Booming mines under people's feet.

People are dying and the economy is dropping,
Governments are falling and people are sobbing,

Men and women with hearts throbbing,
Terrorists make it hard for good governance.

East or west,
Peace is the best,
Try its best and forget all the rest,
Better and best peace is the test.

If all of us have peace,
All the world would be in one piece,
But if there is no harmony,
All nations weep in agony.

We have heard of the bombings,
Of the American Embassy,
We have watched the killings,
Of innocent pedestrians.

Terrorists, it is not hard to make peace,
Love and care is what we need but we miss,
Heart and humanity is what you don't have,
Try your best to stop killing the innocent.

Terrorists, I say, try your best not to kill,
Making people one mighty hill,
To all humans peace is strong,
To all families it is a strong bond.

Peace

Joanne Mteteri

From the east to the west,
Algeria to Liberia,
Niger to Nigeria,
Peace will prevail.

The cunning people,
With raging beliefs,
Hurt poor cripples,
With hoping reliefs.

The atomic and nuclear bombs,
That have high sounds that go boom!
Send thousands of people to tombs,
Leaving the rest doomed.

Misunderstandings and conflicts,
Are the reasons we constantly fight,
And drive us from the light,
When all we want is calm.

The first and second world war,
Left everyone in despair,
Is there another war cooking?
These are words that I can never bear.

Terrorists come to different countries,
Hoping to destroy anything they see,

People die in masses,
We have no choice but to agree.

Many children have to suffer the consequences,
Of the mistakes that most people make,
Never to follow the children's request,
They have to flush their wishes in a lake.

The rate of refugees increases,
Year by year and never decreases,
Hoping someday it will stop,
And the animosity will drop.

Why always fight?
Can't we just stop and think?
Because I see a light,
That shows that we can never sink.

We can live in peace,
As one family,
To make a new dawn,
For everyone around us.

Peace
Namara Lwansa

Oh Peace!
You are something we want
You are not manufactured in a plant
You   are the glue that holds the world.

Oh! Peace,
 You scare away violence,
You are friends with silence,
You are the glue that holds the world.

Oh! Peace,
You are amazing,
You are nothing as bad as over grazing,
You are the glue that holds the world.

Oh! Peace
You are the remedy in a crisis,
 If you were anybody you'd be my sis,
You are the glue that holds the world.

Oh! Peace
You are my joy,
So I don't treat you like a worthless toy,
You are that glue that holds the world.

Peace in the World

Fautia Mogaeka

Peace is an imperative derivation in life,
That doesn't perforate like a knife,
Peace is something that's very fragile,
So it necessitates you to be agile.

Peace depends on a lot of factors,
So please don't be an actor,
Who pretends they discern loads of things,
Meanwhile they're disarraying everything.

Without peace, we encounter a lot of enmity,
So be organized with a lot of dexterity,
For when it strikes you'll never see an indication,
So please listen with a lot of dedication.

Our contemporary world is full of mutineers,
That know very well how to sneer,
My advice is for you to be careful,
Or else you'll end up with a handful.

But truly this is something that irritates,
Because if you ignore it for long, it germinates,
This is really a nonsensical monster,
That causes outrageous disaster.

Thus endeavor to eradicate the encumber,
That is caused when a lot of people plunder,

The solitary thing that glues others mutually,
And facilitates them to subsist peacefully.

My World, My Peace

Jasmine Kapya

Did you know that big things come in tiny packages?
But to my surprise some haven't had it for ages
Something that our souls and hearts mostly desire
That makes us calm and be admired.

When will war end
If there is no one brave enough to stand and defend?
When will terrorism stop?
Is there anyone who knows
Where peace could be bought?

Peace, many are fond of your work,
That keeps many hidden shadows in the dark
Peace you're something we need to acquire
For you're something that keeps us inspired.

We shall fight against violence
And keep hatred wrapped in a pit
Let's join hands and promise to be true
I welcome you Mr Peace.

Printed in the United States
By Bookmasters